Kazumasa Ogawa

Scenes in Nikko and Vicinity

Kazumasa Ogawa

Scenes in Nikko and Vicinity

ISBN/EAN: 9783337300432

Printed in Europe, USA, Canada, Australia, Japan

Cover: Foto ©Andreas Hilbeck / pixelio.de

More available books at **www.hansebooks.com**

Interior Shrine of Igetatsu Haden

Interior Haiden of Iye-yasu Shrine.

Karamon Gate.

Karamon inside.

Side view of Haiden Iye-yasu (a hall for worship in front of a Ma...)

53

Interior Haiden , Oununa .

31

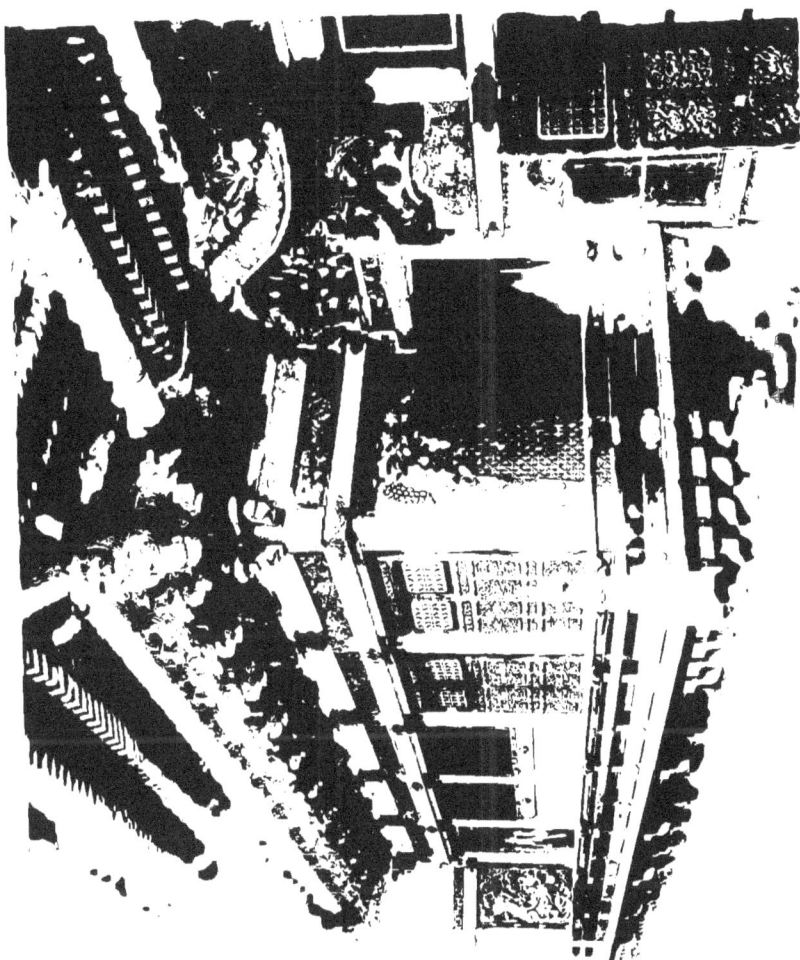

Side view of Huden Iyeyasu.

Interior Haidan (Quinona).

Interior from side view Shrine of Iye-mitsu Haiden

Gate of Chinese woods, from inside Tomb of Iye-mitsu.

Side view Den of (Huden) Shrine of Iye-mitsu

Front view Interior of Iye-mitsu Shrine (Ha-den).

www.ingramcontent.com/pod-product-compliance
Lightning Source LLC
Chambersburg PA
CBHW021610270326
41931CB00009B/1414